MAMA?
MAMA?
MAMA?
MAMA?
MAMA?
MAMA?
MAMA?
MAMA?
MA MA!
Mama!
MA MA!
MAMA?
MAMA?
MAMA
Mama!
MAMA!
Mama!
MAMA?
MAMA?
MAMA?
MAMA?
MAMA?
Mama!
MAMA?
MAMA?
MA MA!
MAMA?
MAMA?
MAMA?
Mama!
Mama!
MAMA?
MAMA?
MAMA?
MAMA!
MAMA?
Mama
MAMA?
MAMA!
MA MA!
MA MA!
MAMA MAMA! MA!
MAMA
MAMA?
MAMA?
Mama!
Mama!
MAMA!
MAMA?
MAMA?

PARENTING.

Illustrated with Crappy Pictures

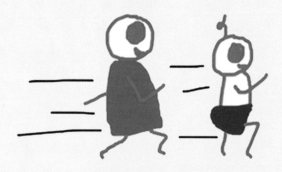

AMBER DUSICK

Parenting: Illustrated with Crappy Pictures
ISBN-13: 978-0-373-89274-7
© 2013 by Amber Dusick

For permission please contact Harlequin Enterprises Limited, 225 Duncan Mill Road,
Don Mills, Ontario, Canada, M3B 3K9.

Library of Congress Cataloging-in-Publication Data

Dusick, Amber.
  Parenting : illustrated with crappy pictures / Amber Dusick.
     p. cm.
  ISBN 978-0-373-89274-7
  1. Parenthood--Humor. 2. Child rearing--Humor. I. Title.
  PN6231.P2D87 2013
  818'.602--dc23
                            2012031901

www.Harlequin.com

Printed in U.S.A.

To my totally noncrappy family and
friends. Thanks for making life so fun.

thank you

CONTENTS

Here is a picture of us so you can see what we look like:

Meet the Crappy Family

Hi, I'm Crappy Mama. I have two kids. I call them Crappy Boy and Crappy Baby because I draw crappy pictures of them. They aren't actually crappy. Not usually. I also have a husband, Crappy Papa.

Right now, Crappy Boy is five and Crappy Baby is two, but many of the stories in this book take place when they were younger. When the story takes place a long time ago, I use past tense. Fancy!

Some of you already know me from my blog, CrappyPictures.com. But if you don't, let me attempt to make a short story even shorter. I started a blog mostly because I was tired and frustrated and happy. I drew some crappy pictures to illustrate the day-to-day things that happen to me as a parent because I didn't have any photographs. That was it. No agenda. I was just having fun.

What started out as just a little silly thing I did for fun has turned into a big awesome silly thing that I still do for fun. Like writing this book! Welcome!

And please keep reading. I suck at writing these intro thingies. It gets better. Promise.

BEFORE &

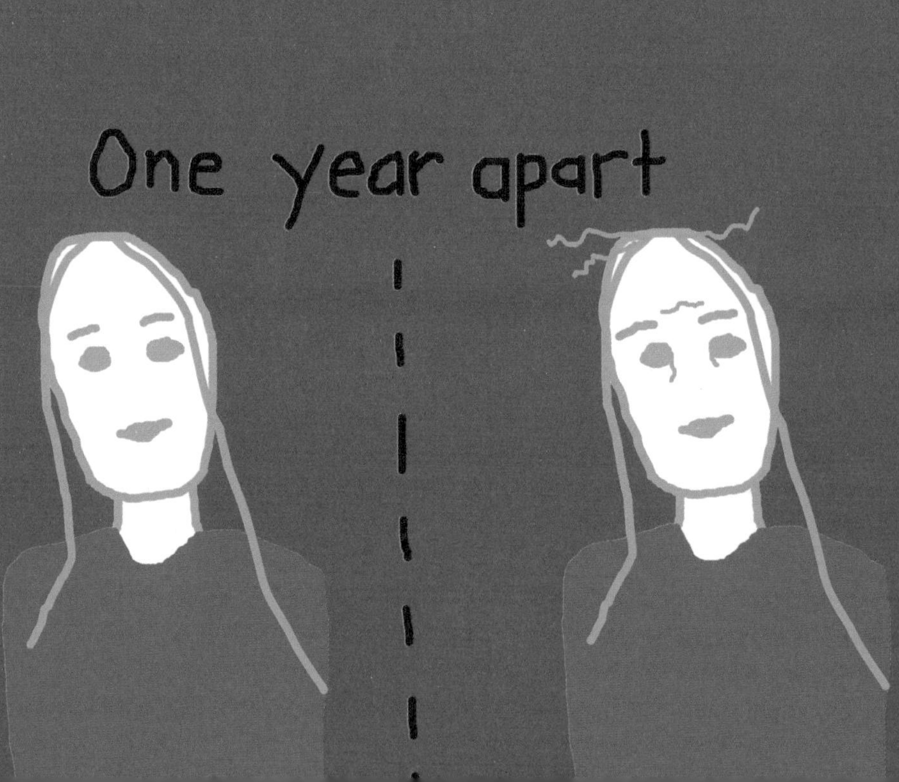

CHAPTER 1

AFTER KIDS

You know what changed after I had kids? Everything.

Most of the changes were good. Very good. They are wonderful little people whom I adore. And I can't imagine my life without them.

But I'm not going to begin this book by talking about unconditional love or any of that boring shit.

I'm going to begin by talking about *other* stuff. Stuff that changed. Stuff like this . . .

AGING

This is what aging was like before I had kids:

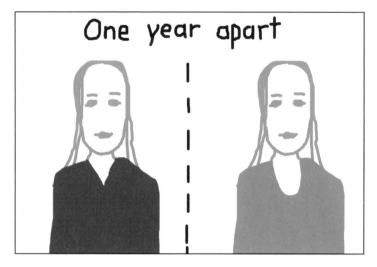

In just one year the only thing that changed was my outfit.

And this is what aging is like after having kids:

Now, I age five years every year.

MY BREASTS

It feels a little premature for me to whip out my breasts. I mean, you are just getting to know me and all. So I'll keep my clothes on. For now.

This is what my breasts looked like before having kids:

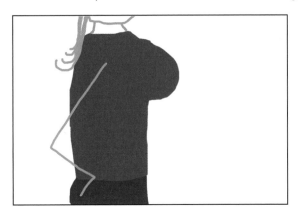

And that was braless. Yes, real. Okay, maybe they weren't that spectacular, but this is how I fondly remember them. (*Fondly*. That looks like I wrote *fondle*. I'm leaving it.)

And this is what my breasts look like after having kids:

Only the most powerful of push-up bras can make them reappear. And I only have *one* of those. So I reserve it for special occasions.

MY STOMACH

This is what it was like to stuff myself before having kids:

I'd feel like I was going to burst!

And this is what it is like to stuff myself after having kids:

My stomach doesn't ever feel like it is going to burst. It just stretches and expands.

He then asked me if it was a girl burrito or a boy burrito. I'm often pregnant with food babies.

There are other physical changes, too. Like peeing from laughing. Yay! And that my feet grew a full size during pregnancy and never ungrew. And that my hair got thinner after pregnancy and never got unthinner. And that my ass disappeared but my hips widened. Oh, and that I also have a little apron of extra skin on my belly. It's cute. And should we talk about my vagina? No, we shouldn't.

But enough of these superficial complaints. Who cares, right? My body made *people*. I'm like a wizard. Wizards don't need perfect bodies because they wear robes. I have a robe. It is purple. *(See how I distracted you from my body flaws by talking about wizards? This always works. Feel free to steal it.)*

There were also changes to my daily routine.

GOING TO THE GROCERY STORE

This is what going to the grocery store was like before having kids:

I could stand there for days, pondering which can of beans to buy.

And this is what going to the grocery store is like now, after having kids:

The only thing I ponder is how fast I can get the hell out of there.

TAKING A BATH

I have always loved to take baths. This is what it was like
before I had kids:

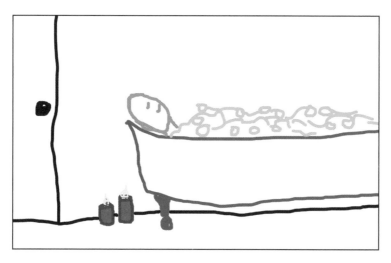

Ahhhh, how relaxing. Candles. Bubbles. Aloneness.

And this is what it is like when I try to take a bath now,
after having kids:

Notice I said *try*. Relaxing bath attempts usually coincide with a crisis on the other side of the door (see Crappy Law #4 in Chapter 10).

Sitting in a waiting room alone used to be annoying. But now it is like a mini-spa vacation. I have to go to the dentist? Yes, please! I fell asleep in the dentist chair last time I went. The dentist was doing something annoying in my mouth like a root canal or something, but otherwise it was awesome. Those chairs are comfy! I never noticed this until after I had kids.

And going to the bathroom has changed, too. No, not the hemorrhoids that I got as a door prize for pushing a nine-pound baby out of my lady hole. The audience. When I do manage to shut the door, it is a very special experience. I read, like, three whole sentences in one sitting. Bliss. Raise your hand if you are in the bathroom right now sneaking a couple minutes of alone time. *(It is kinda my dream that this actually coincidentally works for someone.)*

But this whole before-and-after series would be pointless if I didn't mention the most monumental change of all. Before kids, I knew this change was inevitable and thought I was prepared for it. But this change was a rude awakening. All night long. Repeatedly.

SLEEPING

Sleeping before I had kids:

It was simple. I slept.

This is what sleeping is like now, after having kids:

I don't sleep. And now you can skip the next chapter because you already know what happens.

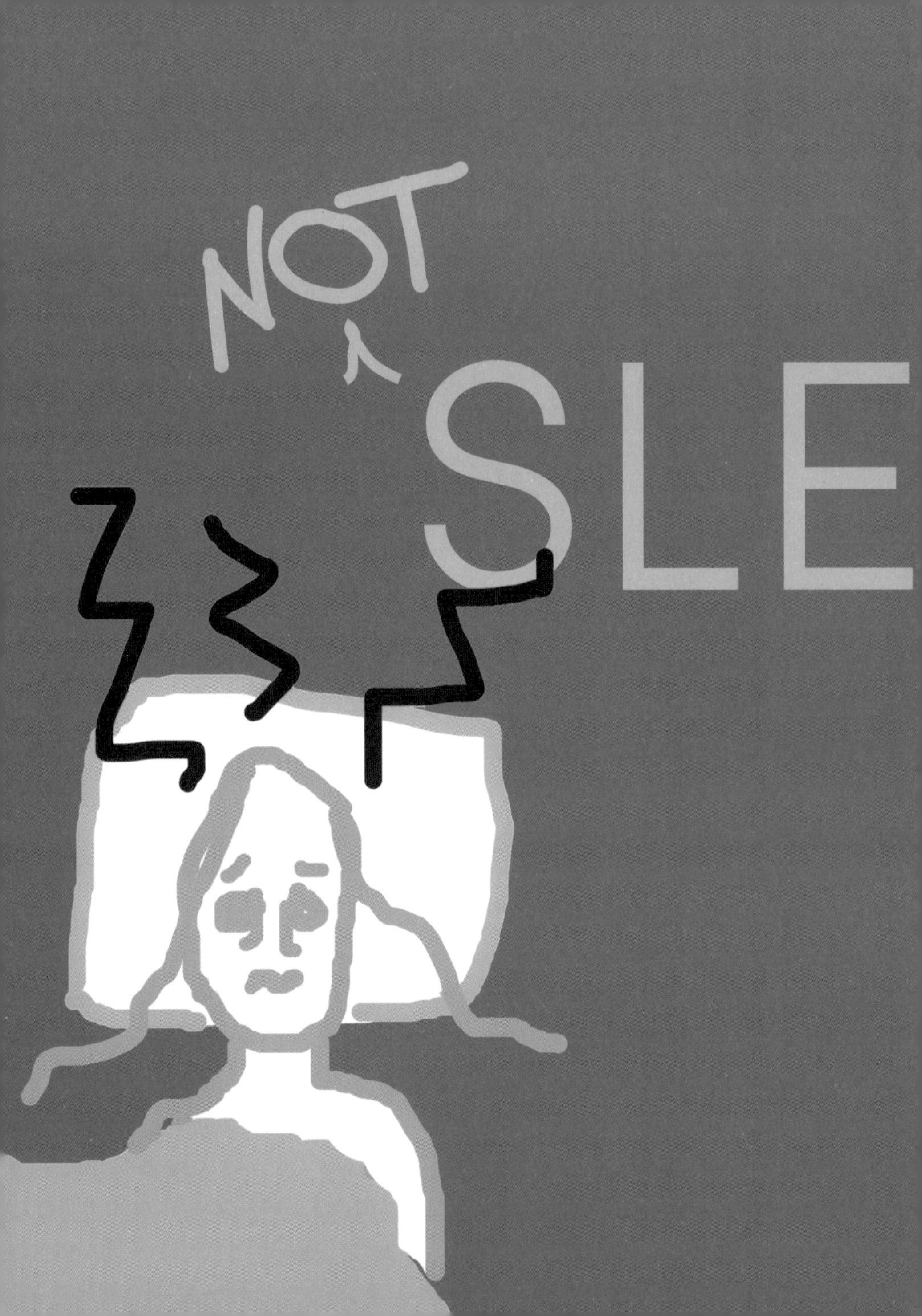
NOT
SLE

CHAPTER 2

EPING

I really should write this chapter but I'm too tired.
The end.

*(Do you think I could get away with this? I'm not lazy.
I'm succinct!)*

All parents complain about the lack of sleep. Why?
Because they all lack sleep.

BABIES DON'T SLEEP

Actually, babies do sleep. A lot. They just do it all wrong.

When Crappy Boy was a newborn, his days and nights were mixed up. This went on for weeks.

Our pediatrician suggested we try to keep him awake during the day to encourage him to sleep at night. Sounded logical. Babies do not give a shit about logic.

No matter what we did to show him that daytime was exciting, he slept. And then all night long he was ready to party:

I know you seasoned parents are squirming in your seats, yelling at me through these pages to, "Sleep when the baby sleeps!" Whatever. No moms ever do this with their first baby because they are too busy looking at the darn thing:

Why didn't I sleep?!

Of course three years later, when Crappy Baby was born, I knew better. I most certainly was going to sleep when the baby slept. Except that I had Crappy Boy to take care of so that was actually impossible. In other words, that advice is lame. Stop giving that advice.

(You may have heard rumors that some babies sleep through the night right away. Just so you know, these are probably lies told by old people to make sure that people keep having babies. If you do have one of those sleeping babies, do not tell anyone! They'll either be jealous or they won't trust you. Or worse. See Crappy Law #41 in Chapter 10.)

PRODUCTS TO HELP TRICK KIDS TO SLEEP

Sleep is such a tiring problem *(Ha! You see what I did there?)* that there are a whole slew of products you can purchase to help alleviate it. It is a huge industry and probably grosses, like, a lot of money each year.

When Crappy Boy was three months old, he was very particular about where he would sleep. He'd be in a very, very deep sleep. So I'd gently, gently lay him down in the co-sleeper right next to our bed:

And he'd wake up. Every time.

The co-sleeper morphed into an overpriced nursing pillow holder. We also had a beautiful crib that he hated. It stored blankets really well. And the cats found it to be quite comfy. They were pretty pissed when we eventually sold it.

We bought swaddling blankets, thinking that they would trick him into thinking he was actually being held or something. The blankets resembled baby straightjackets, but he'd rip his way out of them in about ten seconds:

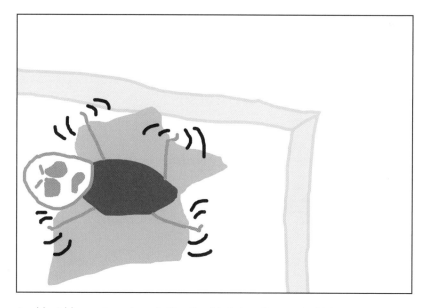

And he'd be extra pissed, like the Hulk busting out of his too-tight shirt.

And that was all we bought. Surprised? Well, we also had a white noise machine, soothing music, soothing lights, a swing and a hammock thing. But we didn't *purchase* any of those. They were all *given* to us by other parents who had already found them to be useless.

The only thing that was actually effective at tricking my babies into sleeping was not something money could buy. It was me. Well, actually it was my milk-producing nipple pacifiers. But we'll say it was me because that sounds cozy.

WHAT IT WAS LIKE TO (NOT) SLEEP AT NIGHT

Then Crappy Baby came along and my not-sleeping habits changed again. Here's what a typical night was like for a while.

We'd climb in bed at 9:00 p.m. . . .

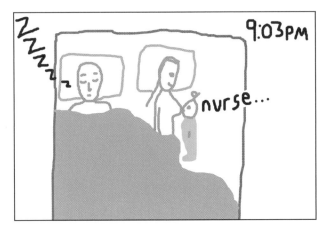

By 9:03 Crappy Papa was completely asleep.

I'd be nursing Crappy Baby and hadn't even begun to think about sleeping yet. I'd lie there motionless, pretending to be calm and relaxed so he'd fall asleep.

I pretended to be sleeping but really I was going over the "to do" list or replaying conversations from earlier. Or I'd have pretend conversations that might happen in the future. On a good night he settled pretty fast.

Finally, around 10:00 p.m. he was asleep. Success! He rolled over and my body was my own for the first time all day. I pulled up the blankets a little. I closed my eyes for real. Started to relax and let go . . .

Until I heard a noise.

Becoming a mama gave me heightened spidey senses. A tiny

noise a mile away woke me up like a mama bear, ready to protect her young.

My husband did not develop this quality with parenthood.

Crappy Boy entered. I thought he was asleep. He had no concept of being quiet while people are sleeping, so he barged in loudly asking for random shit. I had to jump out of bed and rush him out of the room so he didn't wake the baby. This attempt was successful about 50 percent of the time. Let's assume it was successful this night.

So I was in the hallway, hearing Crappy Boy's demands and bargaining with him. Water, bathroom, covers on or off, etc. I had no real power here—I'd agree to anything to get him back in bed quietly. When he exhausted all the standard stuff, he finished by needing to tell me something very important, like "I saw a rock today on the ground and it had dirt on it and I forgot to tell you!" and I steered him back to his room.

By the time I headed back to my bed, the baby had turned into a starfish. Legs and arms stretched out, taking up my whole side of the bed.

I slid next to and under him, being careful not to wake him. I couldn't move. I was scared to breathe. This was a very delicate situation. I had to move him. I had to risk it.

The first attempt to move him just made it worse. He swung both arms and legs on top of me. He was stirring so I couldn't move a muscle. I was like a statue while I listened to his breathing to hear when he was in a deep enough sleep to move him.

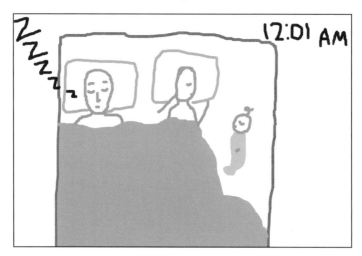

Finally, by midnight I had successfully moved him. I hadn't heard from Crappy Boy in a while so he must be asleep, too. I fell asleep for the first time!

Until I was awakened by a foot in my eye. I tried to ignore it. A foot in the eye was a sign that he was starting to move into a lighter sleep. This meant he'd wake up completely to nurse soon.

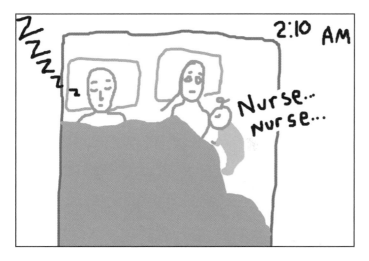

We nursed again. I was half asleep but mostly just felt like a zombie. My mind wandered to weird stuff. I closed my eyes and saw flashes of people and places like a dream, except I was awake.

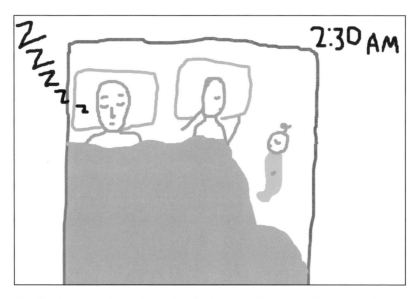

Finally, he settled again and rolled away. It was 2:30 a.m. and I could finally get some real sleep! It was very unlikely that either kid was going to wake me up again. Sweet sleeping bliss.

Until the two cats came in at 5:00 a.m. and announced that they were hungry. They continued to make this announcement every fifteen minutes or so. I ignored them. But they knew. I was their target. They knew I was awake no matter how hard I pretended not to be. They finally settled on my feet so that they would be alerted the moment I stirred. I got a few more minutes of sleep.

Only to be woken up at 7:00 a.m. for a new day. Crappy Boy skipped into our room and gleefully sang, "Morning! It's morning time!" Which woke up Crappy Baby, who replied with "Mownin!"

Then they jumped on our bed.

Even this didn't wake up Crappy Papa. He was still sound asleep.

"Go see Papa," I grumbled.

They had to poke his head and repeat "Papa!" over and over again until he finally woke up.

And what was the first thing out of his mouth?

Grrrrrrrrrrrrr.

THE BEDTIME ROUTINE AND THINGS I DO WHEN I SHOULD BE SLEEPING

Both Crappy Boy and Crappy Baby pretty much sleep through the night now *(Yes, this actually can happen! It isn't a myth!)*, and I have a new, incredible sense of freedom at night.

I'm still tired all the damn time, though. But it's all my fault. Here's why . . .

Every parent loathes the bedtime routine. Actually, there are probably some parents who love the bedtime routine, but I've never met any and they are probably weird.

Why do I hate it so? Because our goals are not compatible. My goal is to get them into bed. Their goal is to avoid getting into bed.

Nightly rituals are employed to let the children know that sleeptime looms. Our ritual has evolved into a complicated and arduous process with many steps. Any mistake in the order or execution of these steps will upset the balance of the universe. And nobody likes that.

Let's assume that even though I'm barely keeping my eyes open, I successfully perform the choreographed dance of teeth brushing, mouth washing, changing into pajamas, peeing, book selecting, book reading, storytelling, back rubbing, question answering, water fetching, forehead kissing, goodnight saying and door shutting. All is quiet. I, too, can sleep.

But this is the first me time I've had all day! I suddenly have a burst of energy! I'm alone and free!

I'll just check my email quickly before I head to bed:

Four hours pass. I've been very productive. Online window shopping for things I will never buy, bookmarking craft projects I will never create and copying recipes I will never make. And now I have to get up in six hours. Oops.

But it isn't always the computer. You know how kids don't want to go to sleep because they fear they are going to miss something? Sometimes they are right. Don't tell my kids.

My husband and I have been using our new freedom to do adult things together:

Like eat massive amounts of junk food while we watch TV.

We know we are taking a huge risk with this behavior. If we ever get busted eating late-night cookies and ice cream, our kids will never sleep again. We've almost been caught:

So we need to get smarter or we will destroy everything. Like our lives.

I also do good stuff late at night. Like write this sentence.

HOW KIDS WAKE UP

The reason it is so excruciatingly painful to be woken up in the morning isn't necessarily because I stayed up too late the night before or because my kids wake up before the sun does.

It is because of the way they wake up. Kids are on–off light switches. They have an off:

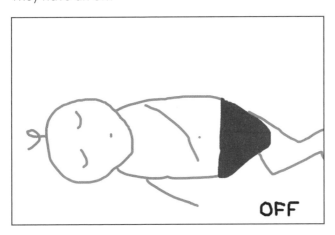

And they have an on:

They can go from off to on instantly.

While me? I am a dimmer switch:

A very slow dimmer switch.

Fueled by coffee.

COFFEE: THE PARENTING WONDER DRUG

I never drank coffee before I had kids. We didn't even own a coffeemaker.

Back in those days, I looked down upon anyone who needed coffee in the morning.

Then I had two kids.

Kids wake up with energy. Kids wake up with loudness.

Kids wake up too fucking early.

No, I will not play with you. Go away. I need coffee.

After coffee:

I don't need it. But *they* need me to have it.

I'll stop drinking it just as soon as they stop waking me up before dawn.

So if anyone ever asks how I pulled off writing a book with two young kids at home, you know the answer. Late nights and drugs. *(I could just say coffee, but answering it this way sounds rockstarish. And really, parents are just uncelebrated rock stars—we stay up late, take drugs and treat our bodies like crap. Yay!)*

And now that this chapter is nearly finished, I will solve all your sleep problems with this brilliant bit of advice (and it isn't even coffee):

Awww, come on, did you really think I had an answer? Nobody does. Yawn. Group hug.

CHAPTER 3

TING

I like eating. My kids sometimes like eating, too.

MY BREAST-FEEDING JOURNEY
(WELL, SOME OF IT)

Before we get to solid food, we should start way back at the beginning. Breast-feeding.

This is what it was like to nurse Crappy Boy:

I'd sit down on the couch to nurse. Crappy Boy would fall asleep. I couldn't move or he'd wake up. I had to pee and I was hungry and thirsty.

We'd often have dinner while he nursed:

Sometimes, I even went to the bathroom while nursing:

In fact, I went everywhere while nursing.

I felt like a ninja.

And this is what it was like to nurse Crappy Baby:

Some babies don't just lie there. No, they like to mess with stuff. Some rub their own ears or hair. Some grab for the other nipple. Some pull off their mother's glasses. And some fiddle with her bra straps. Crappy Baby was a belly button digger. If I forgot to cut his nails, I wound up with little red scratches. But what he really enjoyed was trying to pick my nose and putting his feet in my mouth:

And he'd giggle, while still latched on.

Once he was mobile, he never stopped moving, even to nurse:

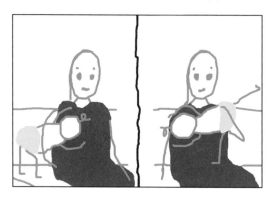

He performed nursing yoga, constantly switching positions. He'd look behind him or around the room. And sometimes he even forgot to unlatch when he got down to play. Despite my increasingly extendable nipples, that actually hurt quite a bit.

EARLY EATING STYLES

Neither of my kids were spoon-fed. It isn't that I avoided it. They did:

So we waited until they were ready to handle it on their own.

Crappy Boy played with his food when he was a baby. He'd smash bananas in his hands. He'd push blueberries around as if he were playing pool with his finger. He was also a dumper. And a thrower:

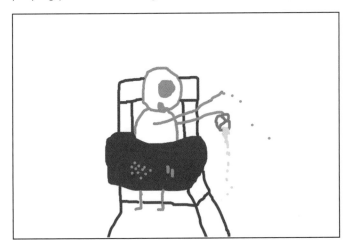

He didn't eat much.

When Crappy Baby started eating food, things were different. He'd put a pea into his mouth. And another and another. He was eating! Then I realized:

He was a chipmunk. He would put food in his mouth and tuck it in his cheek. He didn't eat much, either.

Eventually, he started using a spoon:

And he began to learn the fine line between a bowl and a hat.

Drinking with a straw was a learning process, too:

But the best (and by that I mean the most frustrating) was the way Crappy Boy would tell us he was finished eating. He was talking already so he could have just told us. But instead . . .

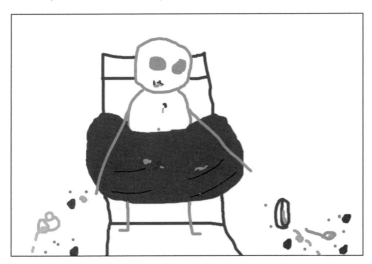

. . . he turned his arms into windshield wipers and cleared the entire tray with two swipes. And *then* cheerily said, "Done!"

FEEDING TODDLERS

After they get the hang of actually ingesting food, kids realize something. That they are in control. Crappy Baby loves this new power and wields it at every chance now.

He wants yogurt. Or "fogurt."

So I open the fridge to find three identical containers of yogurt.

He is peering in behind me and wants to pick.

Yes, they are identical but I'm aware of exercising independence and all that parenting toddlers stuff.

So I pause and let him pick. He grabs the one on the right.

I begin to shut the fridge door, thinking we are done.

Apparently, he has made a mistake. The yogurt on the right is no good.

I put the offending yogurt back and he grabs the middle one.

And throws it on the floor. This one is even more offensive.

So I pick it up, put it back and he grabs the one on the left this time.

And he throws himself on the floor, along with the yogurt. Clearly, the worst yogurt ever.

When he calms down, he goes back to his original choice. The one on the right. A wise choice.

He is happy with his final choice and he is ready to eat it. Except he can't open it.

So I do something stupid. I offer to help.

Eventually, he will realize that letting me help sometimes is actually beneficial to him. Starting at around age four, this independence thing will do a 180. He'll want me to do everything for him, even when he is perfectly capable of doing it himself. I've been told that this stage lasts until they move out. I'll keep you posted.

THE MOST EVIL FOOD FOR KIDS

Crackers are the most evil food. Surprised? You probably thought I was going to say sugar, because it makes kids crazy.

No. The answer is crackers.

Kids like crackers. Parents like crackers because they aren't candy, but are just as easy. I don't trust crackers.

Why? Because crackers create a mess that is larger in volume than the original cracker ever was:

And nobody can explain how this happens.

NEED EAT LIVE!

Humans need to eat to stay alive. So when Crappy Boy doesn't eat, ancient messages echo up from the recesses of my cavewoman mind:

Even though I'm instinctually coded to freak out if my brood is not thriving, I don't panic. (Thriving, *of course, is defined mostly by eating vegetables.*) I don't panic because I know that there is a pendulum that swings between eating air and eating mountains. And it always keeps moving.

During the air stage, he eats almost nothing. Prior favorite foods are snubbed. He will occasionally agree to eat, but he will finish quickly:

But then, suddenly and without warning, he becomes an endless pit and can eat mountains of food:

I enjoy it while it lasts because eventually it switches back. Growth spurt over. He resumes eating air and I resume quieting my inner cavewoman. "Need eat grow!"

DINNER AT HOME

After you have kids, *relaxing dinner* becomes an oxymoron.

We keep trying, though, as we really do enjoy food and long for days when we get to once again, well, *enjoy* it.

As soon as dinner starts, the requests start:

So before I sit down I'm getting waters and various other dinner accessory requests. I ask several times if anyone needs anything else while I'm up. And then I return. And sit down.

Which sparks more requests. Crappy Papa takes a turn to get things. *(By the way, we do gently remind them about saying "please" and stuff. The manners police need not arrest us. I'm leaving out this part because it would take up the whole damn book if I left it in.)* Finally, everyone is sitting and eating at the same time. Until:

Water is spilled and I'm up again to get a towel. Then I clean up and put the towel in the kitchen. When I return and am about to sit down:

More chaos. I'm up anyway so I might as well get the carrots. I bring the carrots to Crappy Boy. He takes one bite and then:

They are both done, even though they really didn't eat much.
They run off to the family room. Finally, a moment of quiet.
I take a couple bites. Only to be interrupted by:

I shovel food in my mouth and drop my plate off in the sink
as I head to the family room to play mediator.

Finally, dinner is over. Then, as I'm washing the dishes:

THE
GOOD

CHAPTER 4

STUFF

What, you thought I'd write a parenting book that was composed solely of my complaints about parenting? That would suck.

I have to make room for some good stuff, too. Especially because I actually love being a parent. *(Don't tell anyone.)* Honestly, even the bad stuff is good stuff when it isn't happening. Remember that. Not that it will actually help you or anything. I just like saying "remember that" because it makes me sound all wise and stuff.

MAXIMUM CUTENESS
(OR, TINY LITTLE MANIPULATORS)

At some point, all babies reach what I like to call the "Maximum Cuteness" stage.

Maximum Cuteness officially starts at sixteen months and lasts until they are three and become assholes.

Crappy Baby is in this stage right now.

Children in the Maximum Cuteness stage have a superpower. Their superpower is the ability to defuse hostile situations. Like a mother's anger, for example.

It is lunchtime. The boys are set up with food. I run to the kitchen to see if we have soy sauce in the fridge. When I return, I find:

Rice. Everywhere. He is actually tossing it into the air!

I'm about to explode with frustration. How can he have made such a huge mess in three seconds? Did a single grain of rice even make it to his mouth? He is making a mess on purpose!

My face looks like this:

A serious hostile situation here.

I interrogate him:

He pauses in his throwing and notices that a hostile situation has developed.

He deploys his superpower.

Okay, this is a little cute. He thinks he is having a celebration.

My brow softens. Waves of heated anger no longer radiate from my scalp.

But I'm still annoyed.

He reassesses the situation. Turns it up a notch.

By saying something even more cute.

Creative grammar always gets me. He must know this.

A half smile even appears.

He sees it and knows he is on the right path. He reaches for his big guns.

And says he is sorry with those GIANT innocent eyes.

And I'm reduced to a loving mother zombie:

Every time.

SHARING THE MAGIC

The best part of parenting is watching kids experience cool stuff for the first time.

We are at a friend's house and they hear the tinkling sound of an ice cream truck for the first time ever. *(No, we don't have them in our neighborhood. It is tragic. We should move.)*

We run to the front yard and it turns out to be a dirty gray van. They are selling treats out of a cooler in the back. This is nothing like the fanciful, polka-dotted ice cream truck of my childhood.

However:

It is just as magical for theirs.

THE COOKIE YEARS

When Crappy Boy was two, he was obsessed with cookies.

One weekend morning we were talking about what we were going to do for the day. Should we go to the park? Or the beach? We needed a plan. He told us his idea:

While this was technically true, we *did* have frozen cookie dough in the freezer. Somehow, he knew.

There was no denying it. Crappy Papa asked him if cookies were his ultimate goal for the day. He paused for a moment and then quickly added:

We somehow knew to cherish the time when just a cookie and a balloon would bring pure joy. He got both that day.

Another day he suddenly started laughing his head off and said:

I asked him why (trying not to laugh) and while nodding enthusiastically, he explained:

Oh. That explained everything.

And yet another day we got home from the market and he looked down sadly and said:

I asked him why he was grumpy. He replied:

I asked him why he was sad and he looked up at me and said:

Now don't go thinking we gave him cookies for breakfast and stuff. No, we didn't start doing that until he was at least two and a half. Doesn't his obsession with them pretty much prove that he only got them as rare and special treats? I think it does. Besides, judgmental people are ugly. Just so you know.

KNOCK, KNOCK! FIRST-EVER JOKES

Crappy Boy was two when he made up his first-ever knock–knock joke:

So hopeful, this joke.

Crappy Baby was also two when he made up his first one:

These will always remain my two favorite jokes of all time.

WHAT *FORTUNATE* MEANS

We went to the post office the other day and I gave my change to a homeless man who always sits outside with a sign. On this particular day, Crappy Boy asked why I gave him my change.

At some point during the car ride home, I must have said something like "giving to those less fortunate" because hours later, that same night, he asks me what *fortunate* means.

I know immediately he is still thinking about the homeless man we encountered earlier.

He isn't satisfied with a synonym like *lucky,* which I attempt at first. No, he needs a deeper explanation.

So I try.

I basically tell him that we are fortunate because we have a home and the homeless man might have to live in a cardboard box.

For a moment, I think I did a pretty good job. But he latches onto the cardboard box idea too eagerly. Too enthusiastically.

And by the look on his face I can tell he has the wrong idea.

So I try again. Further explaining how it would basically suck to be homeless. Being an adult female, I mention not having a bathroom. Obviously.

He asks me where the man goes to the bathroom to clarify.

I could tell I had failed once again.

So I get smarter.

I think about who my audience is. And try again.

Having no freezer in your cardboard box has lots of consequences.

Bingo. He gets it. Fully understands the impact.

So much so that he is downright concerned. And he comes up with his own charitable idea.

And I say, "Sure, we can ask the man if he wants one."

So next time you see a little boy handing an ice cream treat to a homeless man at the post office . . .

Well, that little boy just might be mine.

And *that* is what fortunate means.

PERFECT AND LOVELY

I was getting ready for a rare night out and was putting on makeup in the bathroom. Crappy Boy was watching me, standing on a stool. He was two. I let him put on some lip balm. He asked me if he could also put on some mineral powder foundation and I said:

You don't need it. Your skin is perfect and lovely, just the way it is.

He looked up at me, considered it for a moment and then said:

Mama 'kin perfect and lovely too.

And he gently patted my cheek. I felt beautiful.

I'LL BE THE MAMA

One afternoon when he was almost three, Crappy Boy said:

I pretended to cry and asked for milk. He got it for me from his play kitchen. Then I continued to be a baby in the most annoying yet accurate manner possible:

After that I asked for food, but didn't want the toy carrot he brought. He ran back and forth getting me everything I wanted. He did a really good job being the mama.

But after about five minutes he was tired out and he said:

Damn straight. And don't you forget it.

CHAPTER 5

LING

Before I had them, I always had visions of exploring the world with my children. I love traveling! Just think of how worldly my children will be! They'll learn firsthand about other cultures and eat exotic foods! They'll have a deep understanding of history and geography by visiting different continents! It will be the most amazing thing ever!

Please don't make me travel again.

FIRST AIRPLANE TRIP

Crappy Boy was just three months old when we took him on his first-ever airplane trip.

As we walked toward the security line, he fell asleep all snug in his sling. He would sleep for at least a few hours.

That is, he *would have* slept for a few hours.

I took him out, put the piece of cotton fabric through the x-ray machine and walked through again, carrying the awakened and crying baby. But this time, I had *really* done something wrong.

Only he wasn't wearing shoes. He was wearing socks. I know the shoe rule! I wasn't trying to be sneaky! I tried to point this out but I just got barked at even louder. So I pulled them off and tried to walk through holding the socks. Apparently, that is a huge crime. I thought I was going to be arrested. Instead, the TSA agent made me go back into the line, push through the very, very annoyed people and grab a bin to put the pair of wee socks in for them to scan.

All the while the baby was crying.

Finally, we headed to the terminal and boarded the airplane. When we sat down, I sighed in relief. I got him comfy on a blanket and a rolled-up sweater and I nursed him. He fell asleep. He'd likely sleep for most of the flight even.

Well, he *would have* slept for most of the flight.

The flight attendant was thorough. It must have been her first day. After I lifted the corner of the blanket and showed her that the seat belt was indeed across my lap, she said that she needed to see the buckle. To make sure it was fastened. Which required me to lift up the peacefully sleeping baby. Which startled him and woke him up. Which made him cry. Which made me anxious. Which made him cry more.

I did get him to settle down again eventually and we were left alone for the rest of the flight. No, we didn't wind up being *that* family—the one with the screaming baby on the plane. Not this time. This was actually the least stressful trip we ever took.

OUR CRAPPIEST TRIP

This is the story of our most recent airplane trip.

I hate to complain too much about airplane travel. In my opinion, if you arrive at your destination alive, then you should shut up and be grateful. You could have crashed to your fiery death! Are you alive? Then it was a good flight.

We have been planning for this trip for almost a year. The airplane ride is five hours. Followed by another five hours in a rental car. Our final destination is a secluded cabin in the middle of nowhere. *(Actually, I think it is called "Wisconsin.")*

The night before, Crappy Baby had a poop explosion. It was the worst diarrhea he has ever had. However, it only happened once. The rest of the night was poop-free. *(I describe it more in Chapter 9. I feature this particular poop in two chapters! It is that extraordinary.)*

We load the car to head to the airport. He doesn't have a fever. He doesn't seem sick. Everything seems okay! We drive to the airport. We check our bags, we go through security and we find our gate. We buy sticker and activity books at the store for the kids. We buy snacks. We are totally set and get ready to board the plane.

People mentally clap for us as we entertain our kids while we wait. We are pros. We should teach family travel classes. We've totally got this. Our flight begins to board.

And then Crappy Baby poops.

Putting a disposable diaper on a baby with diarrhea is kinda like putting your thumb over the end of a garden hose.

Crappy Papa rushes to the bathroom to change him. I secretly hope that we miss our flight. We don't.

The plane takes off. We are flying! Now we can relax.

And then Crappy Baby poops.

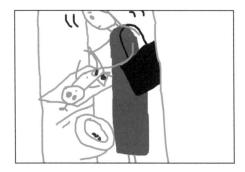

Changing a diaper in an airplane bathroom is like changing a diaper inside an empty refrigerator that a drunk person is pushing around on a dolly.

When we return, Crappy Papa announces that *he* needs to use the bathroom. I see fear in his eyes.

While he is gone, Crappy Boy starts singing a song:

I try to shush him which makes him sing LOUDER!

He also adds crashy explosion sounds.

I can feel the tension of the other passengers. I have to stop this. I quickly suggest a new lyric:

And it works. He continues with the new song and people around us relax their shoulders and even chuckle a little. Sigh of relief. I resume breathing.

Crappy Papa returns. He looks pale. He jokingly asks if I packed any extra pants for *him* in my carry-on. I didn't.

Only two hours have gone by. We have three more to go. We pull out the laptop and watch *My Neighbor Totoro*. Everything is fine.

And then Crappy Baby poops.

And then Crappy Papa poops.

And then Crappy Baby poops.

Finally, the airplane begins its descent.

We made it. The worst is behind us. We get our baggage and take the shuttle to the rental car place. The kids love bouncing around in the shuttle! Yay! The fun begins!

And then Crappy Baby poops.

He has a rash now, thanks to all the pooping. He is grumpy. After having to sit on an airplane for five hours, he now has to sit in a car seat for five more. Poor thing.

Crappy Papa has to make a few hurried bathroom trips before we hit the road.

We load our rental car and install the car seats. We get the kids in. We drive away. Ten minutes later, the car makes a beeping noise and *this* appears on the dashboard:

Or something like that.

So we turn around. Go back to the car rental place. Get back in line. Fill out more paperwork. And get a different car. Another hour has gone by.

Now it is rush hour. It takes us two hours just to get out of the city. We still have four more hours of driving! The kids are starving. We stop to eat. We get back in the car. We drive more. Finally, we're in the countryside. It is dark.

And then Crappy Baby poops.

We pull over and I change a diaper under the stars amid twinkling fireflies. Everyone gets out of the car to stretch and to look at the fireflies. Crappy Boy is entranced. This isn't so bad.

I have to pee. So does Crappy Boy. So does Crappy Papa. We haven't seen a car in miles. I encourage everyone to go ahead. We're in the country now. Nobody cares.

We all start to pee.

Of course, a car drives by at that moment, spotlighting us momentarily with their headlights. An entire family peeing on the side of the road, laughing.

And I realize that it doesn't matter where we are. As long as we're together we're home.

(By the way, we all took turns being sick on that trip. It also rained the entire time, with flooding and road closures. But just forget I told you that part. You can pretend there is a happy ending instead. Which there was—we all made it back home again. Yay! Traveling is awesome!)

THE ROAD TRIP

One year for Crappy Papa's birthday, we decided to go on a road trip from Los Angeles to San Francisco to celebrate.

It is *only* a six-hour drive, we told ourselves. Well, if you don't ever stop. It is actually more like eight hours with kids. Crappy Papa and I feared the drive.

You see, Crappy Baby was at an age (six months) where he really, really hated being in the car. He cried in the car. And Crappy Boy was at an age (three) where he really, really hated just about everything. He only communicated in whines.

We decided to ignore our fears. If we could just get there, then we'd be fine. We loaded the car and did our "Do we have diapers? Books? Thermometer?" cross-check. We expertly calculated the optimal departure time based on nap probability. We even included variables such as Los Angeles traffic and stopping for food.

Everyone was healthy. We had music playlists for both sleeping and awake times. The kids were wearing comfy clothes. The car had been cleaned out and restocked with new toys and books. We had grocery bags full of snacks that they love. We were ready for this expedition.

And we left. With the excitement of the trip, everything went smoothly for at least ten minutes. And then:

Crappy Boy discovered that he was tall enough to kick the back of the seat. *(I'm drawing Crappy Baby forward-facing so we can see him more easily. He was rear-facing back then, obviously. So concerned and/or irate emails regarding car seat safety aren't necessary. Thanks, though.)*

We turned on some music. Crappy Baby started looking sleepy. He quieted and closed his eyes. Then Crappy Boy started yelling again. This woke Crappy Baby up.

So we stopped for food. We filled the car with gas. I nursed Crappy Baby. We got back in the car.

Only five more hours left! They'd fall asleep any minute. We had to be strong.

But Crappy Baby didn't stop crying. His crying intensified. He sounded like he was in pain. I panic. Something was wrong. PULL OVER!

We pulled over on the side of the freeway and I jumped out and got him out of his car seat.

And he barfed all over me. All the milk he just drank was now on me. This meant his belly was now empty again. We nursed in the passenger seat.

When we finished, he was extra pissed about getting *back* into the car seat. For the first several miles it was like this:

Then suddenly, they were asleep.

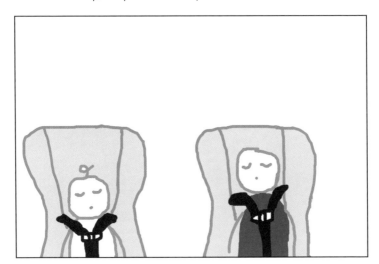

All was well. Deep breath. Until Crappy Papa said:

But we couldn't stop! They'd wake up! Was he crazy? He had to hold it. He should have thought of this before he drank that garbage can–sized soda. I jokingly asked him if he wanted to pee in a diaper. We could *not* stop!

He knew we couldn't stop. They'd wake up if we stopped. But after ten minutes, he couldn't hold it any longer:

So the plan was that I'd hold the diaper for him and he would pee into it. He would concentrate on the road and I would concentrate on making sure the pee actually goes into the diaper. A penis is like a flexible hose. Point the hose at the diaper. Easy.

Only I couldn't stop laughing, which made my diaper-holding skills a little shaky. And then suddenly there was a problem:

A little pee spilled over onto his jeans. I laughed so hard I was crying as I wrapped up the ten-pound diaper. The kids stayed asleep.

I'll skip the part where they woke up and cried for the last two hours of the drive. I'm sure you can imagine it.

We finally arrived. All was well.

The rest of the trip happened. They cried at every restaurant. They cried at everything. I think we had a good time. *(I don't remember. Trauma weakens my memory.)*

Then it was time to drive back home. We were smarter. We were wiser.

Crappy Papa didn't drink soda. I made sure to burp Crappy Baby after nursing. We knew what to expect. We were not afraid.

We were driving through that boring stretch of California near the stinky cow metropolis. It was rural. There were fields. It was raining.

Crappy Boy yelled that he had to poop. Now! There was urgency. We took the next exit. It was called "Just Another Country Road with Nothing Helpful on It" or something like that.

We pulled over next to an alfalfa field. There was *extreme* urgency. Crappy Papa rushed him out of the car and to the side of the road, then instructed him to poop on the ground. Crappy Boy didn't have any shoes or socks on. The ground was muddy. Did I mention the pouring rain? Crappy Papa couldn't put him down.

Crappy Papa yanked down Crappy Boy's underwear and held him above the ground in a sitting position. He immediately turned into a poop dispenser and a pee fountain.

Meanwhile, I laughed my ass off and took pictures through the window of the car. When they returned, they were laughing, too.

Sometimes the crappiest moments make the best memories.

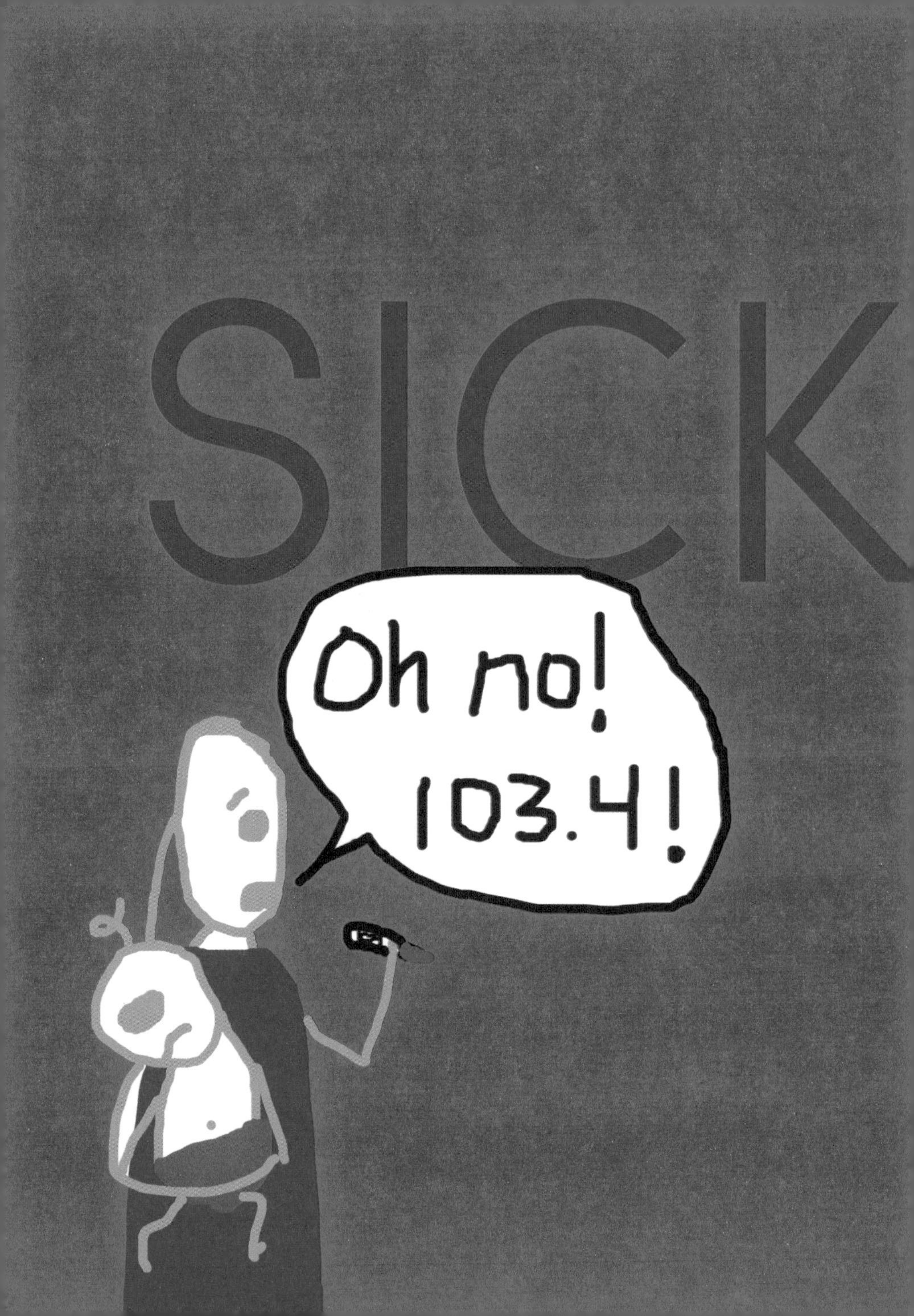
SICK
Oh no! 103.4!

CHAPTER 6

NESS

No matter how tightly I seal the bubble
I keep my children in, they still get sick.

WELL-CHILD DOCTOR VISITS

I hate well-child doctor visits. Especially once I started noticing that my kids would get sick approximately forty-eight hours after their well-child visits. Every. Damn. Time.

Oh sure, the waiting room has a designated "Reserved for Healthy Kids" section, but it is sort of like the division of smoking and nonsmoking sections in an enclosed space.

We have a well-child appointment for Crappy Baby and I am determined that no matter what, they are NOT going to get sick this time.

My plan is to not allow them to touch anything. It is a good plan.

Which fails the moment Crappy Boy touches the door handle. Yes, this is an obstacle I overlooked, but I am still determined to follow the original no-touching plan from now on.

After all, the door handle is not my biggest obstacle. It is the bookshelf.

The bookshelf has three levels. The top two shelves are a jumble of books with tattered and sticky pages. The bottom shelf houses toys. The bookshelf is usually surrounded by kids who most likely have the plague.

Every mother knows that when your child is sick he gets to play with the toys. When your child is not sick, you do everything in your power to avoid physical contact with the toys.

So Crappy Boy takes a few steps toward the bookshelf while I'm signing us in.

Wait, I came prepared! I have stickers, markers, new books and even a small puzzle. Surely I have something in my bag of tricks that will interest him more than the bookshelf.

Nope.

Toys. New toys! He doesn't see the green slime, the cesspool of germs. He doesn't see the sleepless nights with the whining and crying and fevers. He only sees the toys.

I have to come up with something. Fast! Must follow the plan. Time for the big guns.

The phone! I hold it out and wiggle it a little to make it even more enticing.

He takes the bait.

And so we sit for the next fifteen minutes as kids and moms are shuffled in and out of the door. My kids touch nothing. Great success, the plan is working!

Before we know it, they call us back.

I'm feeling so victorious that I don't even tell him to shut the phone off so he can walk properly. Instead, I put my hand on his head, guiding him.

So we get into the examination room. Crappy Boy is still occupied on the phone. The doctor comes in and I'm busy balancing Crappy Baby on the scale.

Crappy Boy says he is done and hands me the phone. He is looking in the full-length mirror.

I pay no attention to the mirror until he puts his mouth on it, doing that thing that kids do where they blow air and make their cheeks puff out.

And I notice how filthy it is. At least twenty other kids before him did this same trick.

I have him sit in the chair and I explain for the millionth time about germs and getting sick.

He listens.

I even notice him nodding a bit when I say *medicine* so I know he understands.

But there was a mistake somewhere in my lecture. Clearly.

He bends over and licks the arm of the chair. Licks it. Like, with his tongue.

The arm of the chair where very sick children have sat and rested their very sick hands.

And he quite happily explains it. He loves medicine!

Right. When *I* was a kid, medicine meant cough syrup that burned my nostrils. But to him, medicine is yummy and comes in fruit flavors.

Plan failed. He ate the germs. I stand there, dumbfounded, and wonder if I should pour hand sanitizer in his mouth. Probably not.

On the way out I stop at the desk to pay the co-payment. The credit card machine isn't working properly so they have to find their manual card swiper. It takes a few minutes.

Crappy Boy gets impatient and turns his gaze once again toward the taboo toys.

This time, though, I just shrug. Why not? He already licked two surfaces. What are a few more germs on his hands going to do?

Sickness is inevitable at this point.

Over the next two days I watch him carefully, looking for signs of illness. But he seems fine the next day. And the day after that.

And the day after that, too. In fact, this was the one and only time he didn't get sick from a visit to the doctor's office.

I guess my plan worked after all.

INDOOR PLAY GYMS

Some indoor play gyms are okay. As long as they hose them down or light them on fire once every few years.

Other ones are breeding grounds for unsavory things. And I'm not just talking about feral kids with no parents in sight. I'm talking about malaria. *(Okay, maybe not that one. But other delightful infectious diseases are available on every surface, included in the price of admission!)*

These places are nasty and I never want to go. My kids love these places and always want to go.

But one day, after an especially rainy month that made for especially stir-crazy kids, I agree to take them.

The gym is an explosion of primary colors and tubes and shapes and soft mats. My kids have happiness seizures upon entering.

On the way in, I notice a sign that says something about their strict sick-child policy. I hope everyone takes note of it.

They remove their shoes while I scan the area for barfing kids to avoid. I notice another sign that says everyone must sanitize their hands before entering the play area. The hand-sanitizing dispenser looks like this:

I think I got typhoid just by looking at it. I operate it using just my elbows.

Hand sanitizer is a total sham. It makes no difference in the face of a coughing kid with green stuff oozing out of her nose, smearing it all over her sleeves. And there is *always* one of those kids.

Crappy Boy runs off to play. Since Crappy Baby is a toddler, I stick around to keep my eye on him.

Once I'm in the play trenches, I notice stuff.

There is a boy grabbing trains away from another little boy, who is crying. And there is a toddler precariously climbing the outside of a tube. Which isn't allowed. There are warning signs posted on the wall. "Do not climb outside of tubes!"

I stand there, wondering:

The toddler has climbed about eight feet high now and is frozen in fear. If he falls he will hit the unpadded metal tube supports all the way down. Not good. His foot slips. I run over in a panic, and glance at the adjacent lounge area where all the parents and assorted caregivers are. Doesn't anyone notice this?

Nope. Nobody is even looking. I help the toddler down to safety and deposit the karma tokens into my account.

But this isn't why I dislike indoor play gyms. This is why I dislike them:

I spot a girl with a snotty nose. She is hacking and coughing, too.

She also happens to be the child that my kids choose to play with.
Sigh.

Her mom comes over and I offer her a tissue for her daughter.

She responds in the usual way:

Yeah. Whatever.

On the way out, we make a pit stop at the hand sanitizer even though I know it is futile.

When we get home, I bathe them in bleach. But it doesn't matter. Two days later:

Two hours at an indoor play gym paid for with several days' worth of illness. No. Not worth it. Indoor play gyms are a rip-off.

THE ENTIRE CRAPPY FAMILY GETS SICK

I hate it when this happens.

I hear them from the kitchen where I'm making breakfast. Yelling. Fighting.

I peek around the corner and discover them using a xylophone mallet and a maraca to hit each other. Because this is what xylophone mallets and maracas are used for. As clubs.

What is the deal? I'm getting grumpy. Why are they being so crazy?

And then, several hours later, I see what the deal is.

They are getting sick.

No matter what the virus is, Crappy Boy gets a stomachache and Crappy Baby gets a runny nose. I never know what it is going to morph into. This is the fun part. The waiting game.

And now my mama guilt is in full force for thinking they were acting like little jerks earlier. For not seeing what was really going on. The poor babies are sick!

The nurturing super mama has taken over.

I'll do anything for them.

And I'm optimistic. I truly believe that if we just have a mellow day full of cuddles and reading and soup, they will get better before they get worse.

Just a quick twenty-four-hour bug. I can handle this.

It seems to be going well. They don't seem to be getting worse.

Until the sun goes down (see Crappy Law #39 in Chapter 10).

Nighttime brings out the worst. Always. I dread the nighttime when they are sick.

But I can handle this. I clean it up and comfort him.

An hour later I'm in the living room walking Crappy Baby back and forth. Crappy Boy is asleep on the couch, wanting to be near me. All is quiet and I think we have seen the worst of it.

And then this happens:

And continues to happen. All night.

Nobody sleeps. Crappy Papa is in the background, mostly on cleanup duty. And thermometer duty. And getting them to drink water duty. He sleeps in between.

Puking. Pooping. Sometimes alternating. Sometimes at the same time.

More puking. More pooping.

More forcing them to drink water. Temperature taking. Carrying. Walking.

Finally, the sun rises. All is calm. We are lying on the floor, flanked by a roll of paper towels and a puke bucket.

I feel a great sense of relief with the presence of the sun. I know the worst is behind us.

This time, I'm right. They remain terribly ill and grumpy and clingy, but the pukefest is mostly over. We lay low all day. They even mostly sleep through the night! Mostly.

Now Wednesday is here and things are looking even better!

Oh, except for me. Once the kids are better, I suddenly remember that I, too, exist on the physical plane and I realize that, wow, I'm super sick. I was so busy tending to them that I didn't even notice that my temperature is 104.

I am the type of sick person who would prefer to hide under the covers and sweat it out. Alone. If I were an injured wolf, I'd go off and die alone in the woods. Alone. *Alone* is the operative word here. Alone is what I need to get well.

Alone isn't going to happen.

They sense my desire to be alone, which makes them cling to me.

But Crappy Papa will help.

Only they don't want him. They want Mama. Only Mama. They still aren't 100 percent themselves and are in that "I was just sick so now I'm super whiny, pick me up" stage of getting better.

Finally, he lures them away from me with promises of playing Candy Land.

Game in progress, I retreat to my bed.

This is the first time I've wished for a never-ending game of Candy Land.

I don't get my wish.

They are back.

Crappy Baby wants to nurse. He is still not feeling well. I get it. But I may have to puke or run to the bathroom with explosive diarrhea. Again. I'm feverish and delirious. It feels like he is draining life out of me.

I just really want to be alone. But I can handle this.

Crappy Papa manages to pry them from me again.

When all is said and done, I think I got about an hour total of quiet alone time. Which is pretty good.

Over the next couple days, I slowly start to get better.

The boys are back to their highly energetic selves and I try to keep up, even though I can barely stand up.

I can handle this, though. I can. We are almost in the clear now.

The weekend arrives and with it, health! We are ready for a fun, family-filled weekend. Nobody is sick so we can actually go places!

The sun is shining! Yay!

And then . . .

He gets sick. On the weekend. How very convenient for him. I try not to be bitter. He really doesn't have control over the timing. At least I don't think he does.

So he proceeds to spend an entire day in bed. Alone.

Moaning.

The kids are stir-crazy, so I take them out of the house. All is quiet and peaceful for him. How nice.

And then he proceeds to spend a second day in bed. Alone.

At some point, as usual, he thinks he is dying.

And so I respond the way I always do.

We've been down this road before. I can handle this.

I tell him matter-of-factly that he is not dying. He just has the flu.

The same flu, I remind him, that I had while taking care of the kids all week.

This is where he is supposed to have an epiphany of how amazing I am and what a hard week it has been for me and why I'm ever-so-slightly annoyed and jealous that he has been in bed for two days.

Only he doesn't.

Instead, he says something that is so completely the opposite of what I was expecting that I'm stunned.

He tells me he must have a stronger, mutated version of the virus. Because there is no way I'd have been able to take care of the kids if I felt even close to how he feels.

I don't even know what to say at first.

And then I know exactly what to say.

So jokingly, I agree with him and tell him that, indeed, he must have a mutated version and that he will probably die. And then I laugh all the way to the kitchen to get him some soup.

See? I *can* handle this.

TOYS

CHAPTER 7

& PLAY

Kids love to play. Kids love toys.
Me, too. Well, mostly.

THE CHIMNEY SWEEP

Crappy Boy likes to pretend. Hard. He was once a robot for three consecutive days. And one time, when he was four, he was a chimney sweep for nearly two weeks.

It started out innocently enough. He wanted to be a chimney sweep. Not just any chimney sweep. He wanted to be "Dick Van Dyke acting the part of Burt, the chimney sweep" from *Mary Poppins*. Okay then.

First, he found a black hat in the dress-up box. Then he convinced me to put a little black mineral makeup on his face and shirt for soot. Why not? He was fully transformed:

It was hilarious. And he was so happy! The next day he did the same thing. And the next. He went about his days "as a chimney sweep" only. We went out to a restaurant. We went to the market. We went about our normal business and I got used to having a chimney sweep for a son. Soot and all.

A week later, I had to return something at the mall and I took him with me. I didn't for a moment even think about what he looked like.

We were standing in line. The woman in front of us turned around with an absolutely horrified look on her face:

She asked what happened. I turned around and looked behind me. I had no idea what she was talking about or if she was even talking to me.

She nearly collapsed with concern as she said:

I was still confused. I looked around for Crappy Baby, thinking that he probably did have a bruise or two from falling down since he is still pretty wobbly on his feet. Only he wasn't even there. He was at home with Crappy Papa. I must have looked either crazy or just very stupid.

Then I realized what she was talking about.

She reached in her purse, probably for her cell phone to call Child Protective Services.

Crappy Boy cheerfully told her that he sweeps chimneys. That didn't help. Quickly, I explained that it is just makeup.

It was just pretend! Finally, she believed me. Her brow softened and we both laughed and talked about *Mary Poppins*.

(He continued to be a chimney sweep for another week after this. She was the one and only person who reacted this way. Most people asked if he was in costume for a play. To which I replied yes. Because that was just easier.)

BOYS VERSUS GIRLS

My best friend, Wendy, and I had our first babies around the same time. She had a daughter. I had a son.

As new moms, we heard tons about "gender stereotyping" and how that was, like, bad and stuff. Saying things like "Boys will be boys" was old-fashioned and frowned upon. We were modern! We would never think or say such a thing.

It was awesome that Crappy Boy loved fairies. It was awesome that her daughter loved pirates. She bought her daughter trucks. I bought my son dolls. We sheltered them from messages that put value on their interests or skills based on gender expectations.

And they do have skills.

Her daughter can turn anything into a baby.

And my son can turn anything into a weapon.

THE SHARING EXPERIMENT

One toy and two children is a recipe for war. This is how war was invented.

My kids would fight over dog shit if there was only one pile of it available.

Some parents wind up buying multiples of the same toy just to avoid this conflict. I didn't ever want to do this, partly because I think they need to learn to deal with conflict and partly because I think it is a waste of money. But finally, I decided to give it a go. Just as an experiment with something small.

I buy two yellow cars. They are identical. I give them only one at first, to test their interest:

They start fighting over it. So I whip out the second one:

I expect that at any moment they'll start fighting over who gets to play with both cars at the same time. But they don't. They pause for a few moments. Silently.

Maybe those other parents were right! Maybe they'll both be content having their own car. Maybe this really is the solution!

But then this happens:

Sigh.

JUMPING ON THE BED

Jumping on the bed is fun! I mean bad. Jumping on the bed is bad. Parents are supposed to teach their kids not to do it. There is even that monkey song to help us. You know, the one where the monkeys hurt their heads and call the doctor and all that?

Jumping. Ten seconds later:

Crying. Ten minutes later:

Those monkeys never learn.

THE REPRODUCTION OF TOYS

We have a serious toy overgrowth problem in our house. This is because toys can reproduce like weeds. They do it when we aren't paying attention.

Children are also to blame because they help with propagation.

They introduce toy species into nonnative habitats.

These toys are invasive. They ruin the landscape and even cause harm to the resident mammals.

The only way to stop the reproduction of toys is to . . .

Never mind, there is no known method. Scientists were working on it, but lost their funding.

LANG

CHAPTER 8

Because blah blah...

I don't know.

UAGE
(IS COOL)

Kids are funny.
Especially when
they start talking.

THE PEACOCKS AT THE BOTANICAL GARDENS

Crappy Baby loved birds when he was just over a year old. So we decided to go to the local botanical gardens to show him the peacocks that roam the gardens. He knew a handful of words at this point, things like *Mama, Papa, meow, baa, duck,* etc. We arrived and entered the lush green landscape.

We spotted a group of peacocks and pointed them out to him. Excitedly, he yelled:

Which he proceeded to do all day long, even after we left the gardens. At *every* bird. And at *every* person. Really, at anything at all that looked interesting. No matter how much we emphasized the *pea* part of the word, he kept saying the same thing.

Yes, one of our younger son's first words was *cock*. Awesome.

CUTE MISUNDERSTANDINGS

After the words come phrases. And those are just as much fun, in a different way.

My mother-in-law was playing catch with Crappy Boy when he was two. Well, there was no actual "catching" going on, but there were attempts at it. She advised him to "Keep your eye on the ball" and:

He put the ball on his eye.

Another time he was terribly disappointed in the extreme lack of fairies on a ferryboat. I can just imagine what he had in mind:

The real thing paled in comparison.

And I'll never forget the time when I was hugely pregnant with Crappy Baby. We were talking about how he was going to be born soon.

Crappy Boy looked worried. Scared even. I was concerned that it was jealousy or fear of the new baby replacing him. So I asked him what was wrong. With tears in his eyes, he said:

Turns out he thought I had said, "So we can *eat* him." *(Back then I chose to believe his reaction was because he felt protective of his brother even before he was born. But now I wonder if it was because he was going through a picky eating stage.)*

GETTING THE MAIL

We heard the mail carrier drop mail into the slot. I opened the front door and explained to a two-year-old Crappy Boy that I was also checking for packages, since I was expecting one. As I started to close the door, he asked, "Any packages, Mama?"

CARLSBAD

We were driving to Carlsbad, California to see our cousins. In the car, Crappy Papa and I were talking about Carlsbad. From the back seat, three-year-old Crappy Boy said,

FRIENDSHIP PILLOW

My mother-in-law had a heart-shaped pillow hanging on a closet doorknob with the word *Friendship* embroidered on it. When Crappy Boy was two, she told him what it said and asked him if he knew what *friendship* meant.

SWEARING

Yes, I swear. Even around my kids sometimes. Go ahead, take away my parenting permit.

There are a lot of things that are worse than swearing.

Still, I try to not swear much around them. And honestly, we're doing something right because *they* never swear. Well, except for those three times.

Crappy Boy was eating peas in his high chair. Well, he was potentially eating peas but he wasn't actually eating. He was two. We were arguing about the temperature of the food.

I will admit a little tiny morsel of pride that he did use the word correctly at least. That same week, he randomly walked into the room and announced:

He really didn't. He had quite an acorn collection already.

More recently, I was driving in the car and muttered "Oh shit" under my breath when I saw the traffic on the freeway. Crappy Baby asked me what I said. I lied. I told him I said "Oh dear." He replied with:

Miraculously, they never repeated those words again. Probably because I managed to adequately stifle my laughter.

PENIS PIZZA

One night recently, we ordered pizza. Crappy Boy and Crappy Baby were in the tub.

Crappy Papa is in the bathroom with them to make sure they don't drown each other or crash tidal waves across the floor.

The doorbell rings. Pizza delivery man is here.

Normally, I'd make Crappy Papa handle these things. You know, human interactions. But he is on tub duty so I'm stuck answering the door. The kids are happily singing a song.

I open the door. The pizza delivery man hands me the pizza box. Now I notice what the kids are singing:

I'll ignore it—that is what I'll do! If I act as if I can't hear it, then he won't be able to hear it, either.

I take the pizza box. Normally I'd walk five steps and set it on the table, but there is no time for that today. I toss it down onto the floor. Uh-oh, that probably looked weird. Now he knows I'm rushing. He knows that I can hear *penis, penis*, which means he can hear it, too.

This makes me uncomfortable. We'll have to do this quick!

The kids start yelling PENIS! over and over again.

Crappy Papa knows I'm handling pizza dealings. He shushes them. Which makes everything worse.

Kids can smell parental embarrassment the way dogs can smell fear.

They start screaming PENIS PENIS PENIS at the top of their lungs with shrieks of laughter in between.

The pizza delivery man hands me the receipt to sign. (PENIS! PENIS!)

Should I say something? Should I make a joke about the kids? Is ignoring it better? I can't think of anything funny to say! (PENIS! PENIS!)

(PENIS! PENIS! PENIS!)

I look at the total and have to decide how much tip to give. (PENIS! PENIS! PENIS!)

I frantically sign it and hand it back and throw the pen at him. (PENIS! PENIS!)

Crappy Cat runs to the door and attempts to bolt outside, but I stop him by stepping on him with my foot. (Gently. Relax, Cat Freaks.)

I'm embarrassed and acting so odd that he must think I'm absolutely crazy. Which I am, but I don't want other people to know.

Balancing on the cat, I manage to say thanks and shut the door.

I will now LOUDLY yell to the kids that the pizza is here and to get out of the tub. I'll intentionally do it loud enough so that the pizza delivery man walking down our porch steps will hear it. This will reassure him that everything is totally normal in our house. That this whole thing has left me unfazed. Just a regular mom with silly kids.

So I yell something. Just not the right thing.

Yes. I yelled that.

I will never answer the door again.

MY FAVORITE

But of all the funny and clever things they've ever said, my favorite is simple. And it is even the same thing for both kids:

Language doesn't get any better than that.

CHAPTER 9

DIAPERS

Poop is funny!

SO MUCH POOPING

When Crappy Boy was a week old, I had no idea what I was doing. He pooped. And he pooped. And he pooped. It seemed like he was pooping every five minutes! Probably because he *was* pooping every five minutes.

It went like this . . .

He pooped. I took off his dirty diaper and cleaned him up. He was starting to get a little red. Oh no, a rash already? Must be from all the pooping. I had to put a little diaper cream on him. I started to apply it gently with my finger and:

He pooped all over my hand. And the new diaper. And the changing mat.

So I started over with more wipes. Finally, I got a fresh diaper on. As I gently pressed down to fasten the tabs:

He pooped again. And again.

Fortunately, this phase didn't last. Eventually, he pooped less frequently. Like once every *six* minutes instead of five.

DIAPER TREASURE

Crappy Baby is in a diaper-stuffing stage. Nearly every diaper change contains a hidden treasure. Sometimes it is just a handful of sand. Sometimes it is a sticker. Or a small toy. Or a rock. Or crackers.

One time I found something good:

So *that* is where it went.

ELEPHANT POOP

So it is the day before we leave for a trip. *(Yes, the "Crappiest Trip" that I describe in Chapter 5.)*

It is early morning and we haven't started packing yet. I walk into the family room and smell . . . something. Crappy Papa notices it at the same time.

He says it smells like dead animals. What could it be? It does not smell like poop. It is too atrocious. Too rotten.

But when there is an unidentified stench in the vicinity of a diaper-clad baby, I automatically check. I have to.

Crappy Boy jokingly asks if he pooped dead animals, because of what Crappy Papa said.

And Crappy Baby answers affirmatively. Excitedly.

Says he pooped elephants. We all laugh. I'm a little worried that this is a clever way of saying he pooped a ginormous amount.

But the diaper is clean.

I declare "no poops" and he responds merrily with "just toots" and we carry on. The smell has dissipated so we forget all about it.

That evening, while getting pajamas for the boys after their bath, I'm interrupted by the call of doom. "Uh-oh!"

I enter the dining room and Crappy Baby is sitting on a chair. Naked.

The stinkiest elephant diarrhea. All over the upholstered chair. And table. And him.

We scrape off the excess and clean up the mess. We go on our crappy trip. (See Chapter 5.) And then we return.

A few days after our return, I think back to the "Elephants!" scene that preceded everything. It was the ominous foreshadowing. Now that it is all over and everyone is healthy, it is actually kinda funny.

The rest of the family is in the other room playing a game, and I'm washing the dishes. Crappy Baby walks in.

He says, "Uh-oh" and grabs at his diaper with a distressed look on his face.

So I ask him if he pooped.

He answers with hippos. Hippos!

I panic.

Are you kidding me? We just got home and just got over being sick. How can this possibly be happening again?

I pick him up and carry him with the "Hold-the-baby-as-far-away-from-you-as-possible-because-you-know-the-poop-is-going-to-ooze-out-all-over-you" technique. I know it is going to be massive.

I see something drop out of his diaper.

But when it lands, the sound is unexpected.

It sounds hard. Really hard. And it rolls.

Perplexed, I set him down gently to inspect.

And five little balls from the Hungry Hungry Hippos game drop out while he pulls at his diaper and bounces.

The game they were playing in the other room? Hungry Hungry Hippos.

TODDLER DIAPER CHANGES

Diapering a toddler is a different animal. An animal with much bigger and stinkier poops.

Toddler poopy diaper changes are a two-person job, but I'm often understaffed.

First, a scent is detected:

He says no to everything so he is not to be trusted.

I go for a visual check by pulling the back of his diaper away from his body:

Being careful to only grab the outside of the fabric, just in case the poop has gone all the way up his back. As usual.

I have to get a visual to determine the severity of the poop. This information is used to estimate how many wipes I'll need to prepare.

It is severe.

I go and wet several with warm water and then plant the wipes in the changing area and find Crappy Baby.

I don't even have to say anything. He knows that it is diaper–changing time. So he runs:

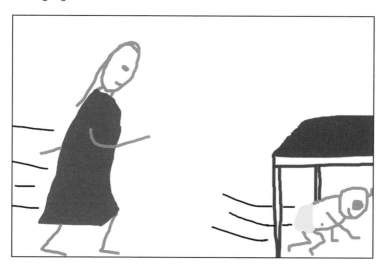

And usually winds up ducking under the table.

And no amount of coaxing will make him budge. I have to drag him out as he giggles. He finds all of this hilarious.

We arrive at the diaper-changing area. I'm totally prepared with wipes, a fresh diaper and a variety of distraction material.

But sometimes I'm not prepared for his leg-swung-over-his-body flip maneuver:

And he escapes!

So I have to hold him down with one hand while selecting a distraction object. I hand him a book.

It is a new book. Not new to our house but new to the distraction offerings basket.

So it actually works:

I move at lightning speed, unsnapping the diaper and grabbing wipes. Holding his ankles with one hand and wiping with the other.

Almost there! This is going well . . .

Book is tossed. His hands go straight to the poop:

Like a ninja, I grab a second distraction object—a duck. I do this using only my mind because I can't let go of his legs.

I offer it in an excited, high-pitched tone so that it sounds fantastically interesting. He takes it. But it too winds up where I don't want it:

Fortunately, he is pretty clean already.

All that is left is to get a new diaper on him. He really hates this.

He backbends, he twists, he flails his arms and legs.

I have to hold him down with my knee:

And finally . . . done! Until the next poop.

POOP IS SPECIAL

Potty training is funny. But I'm not saying it is fun. Those are two different words.

Crappy Baby is fascinated by his poop in the toilet. And it makes sense. When his poop appears, he receives applause and smiles and high fives. Poop must be special!

Crappy Baby is sitting on the toilet and asks me:

He is asking me what the name of his poop is. I tell him it doesn't have a name. It is just poop. He gets very upset about this, so I decide to play along.

I suggest George.

He looks down into the toilet for a moment and then finally says:

He then dumped it into the toilet, and sadly said goodbye to Floofy.

Yep, poop is special.

THE 50 CRAPPY
LAWS OF

CHAPTER 10

PARENTING

By now you might think I'm some kind of parenting expert. I am. Since I'm an expert, I've made a list of parenting laws based on my scientific research.

Up Up

The moment the baby finally falls asleep for a nap, the doorbell will ring. Followed by the phone. And the dog barking. And the older child yelling.

2

The more excited you think they'll be about a gift, the more they will only play with the box.

The colder it is, the more they will NOT put on a sweater.

The closing of a bathroom door causes end-of-the-world panic.

5

If you are sweeping, the only path they can take is
right through the pile.

6

If you are extra tired, they will pick the longest book from the shelf for bedtime.

7

The very first time a child dons new clothes,
they will be stained forever.

8

When you tuck them into bed, they will inevitably (and all of a sudden) become very hungry and very thirsty and also have to pee.

When you make their favorite meal, they won't eat it.

After a long car drive during which you hoped they would nap, they fall asleep a mile from your destination.

The more you are running late, the more poop happens.

A baby can't use a spoon or tie his shoes, but he can delete applications from your phone.

13

The more important a phone call is, the louder they become.

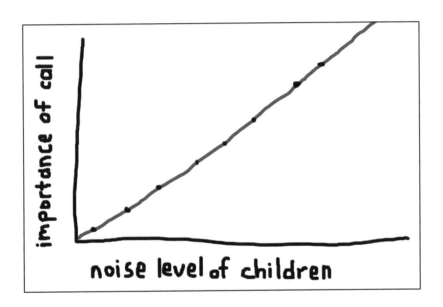

The moment you sit down to eat a nice dinner, the baby will poop.

The more things you are carrying, the more desperately they will require being picked up.

When you sneak to the pantry to eat chocolate, you will get caught.

They will always select the most dangerous object
to pull out of the cupboard.

And they'll pick up the most fragile item in a room.

19

When you hope for a quick nap, they will sleep for hours. When you hope for a long nap, they won't nap at all.

20

A baby will always find something disgusting to put in his mouth, no matter how much you clean or babyproof your home.

21

The one thing you forget to bring is the one thing they ask for.

22

The presence of a video camera immediately eradicates any talent they were just demonstrating.

23

Projectile vomiting is real. (What, this isn't a Crappy Law?
Trust me. It is.)

24

The later you go to bed, the earlier they will
wake up the next morning.

25

The better children behave for someone else, the crazier they will be when they come home.

26

Two (or more) kids will never nap at the same time.

27

Babies only poop on a newly changed diaper, immediately after a bath or when the diapers and the diaper bag are in the washing machine.

The one and only item they are willing to eat
is the one you just ran out of.

Symptoms disappear when you go to the doctor.

30

They will repeat things at inappropriate times.

Food is 100 percent more appealing when it is on the floor or on someone else's plate.

32

If you need to get something done during naptime,
it is guaranteed that they will not nap.

33

On mornings you need to go somewhere, they must be dragged
out of bed. On weekends, they wake up before sunrise.

Kids always get sick right before a family vacation
or a parent date night.

35

The one day you only brought three diapers along is the day they will poop four times.

36

They will want their rejected food back right after you finish eating it.

37

When they vomit, it will most likely be on you.

38

Art supplies are used on everything except paper.

39

They only spike a fever after the sun goes down
and the doctor's office is closed.

40

They always pick the best words to parrot.

If you ever tell another parent that you don't have a problem with something, you will begin having that problem tenfold.

Dressing them in a Halloween costume or layers of winter clothes is directly correlated with their need to pee.

No matter how much you feed them before you leave, the moment they arrive somewhere they will be starving.
Especially if there is no food.

44

The baby will fall asleep on you, but only when you have to pee.
Very badly.

45

When you need space, they will cling to you. Physically.

46

If you toss out that half of a plastic Easter egg they got three years ago, they will notice.

The only toy they are interested in is the one
the other kid is playing with.

They do not censor their words or their volume. Especially in public.

The moment you are about to snap, they say something adorable.

50

Which brings me to the last and perhaps the most important law of all. They will never stop surprising you. The moment you think you have them figured out . . . you don't. And that is awesome.